MIDLOTHIAN PUBLIC LIBRARY

3 1614 00153 8983

DEC 2012

P9-CCG-943

MIDLOTHIAN
PUBLIC LIBRARY

ORIGAMI

easy
ORIGAMI

by Mary Meinking

MIDLOTHIAN PUBLIC LIBRARY
14701 S. KENTON AVE.
MIDLOTHIAN, IL 60445

Capstone
press

Mankato, Minnesota

Snap Books are published by Capstone Press,
1710 Roe Crest Drive, North Mankato, Minnesota 56003.
www.capstonepub.com

Copyright © 2009 by Capstone Press, a Capstone imprint.
All rights reserved. No part of this publication may be reproduced
in whole or in part, or stored in a retrieval system, or transmitted in any form or by any means,
electronic, mechanical, photocopying, recording, or otherwise, without written permission of the publisher.
For information regarding permission, write to Capstone Press,
1710 Roe Crest Drive, North Mankato, Minnesota 56003.

 Books published by Capstone Press are manufactured with paper containing at
least 10 percent post-consumer waste.

Library of Congress Cataloging-in-Publication Data
Meinking, Mary.
    Easy origami / by Mary Meinking.
    p. cm. — (Snap books. Origami)
    Summary: "Step-by-step instructions for easy origami models including a drinking cup, a spinning top,
and a fortune-teller" — Provided by publisher.
    Includes bibliographical references and index.
    ISBN-13: 978-1-4296-2020-8 (hardcover)
    ISBN-10: 1-4296-2020-X (hardcover)
    1. Origami — Juvenile literature. I. Title. II. Series.
TT870.M4325 2009
736'.982 — dc22   2008001677

Editor: Kathryn Clay
Designer: Bobbi J. Wyss
Photo Researcher: Dede Barton
Photo Stylist: Sarah L. Schuette
Scheduler: Marcy Morin

Photo Credits:
All principal photography in this book by Capstone Press/Karon Dubke
Capstone Press/TJ Thoraldson Digital Photography, steps (all)
Syd Spies, 32

The author would like to dedicate this book to: Scott, Britt, and Ben for your loving support and encouragement
as my writing career unfolded.

Printed in the United States of America in North Mankato, Minnesota.
012012
006552R

TABLE OF CONTENTS

page 8

page 20

page 26

INTRODUCTION

Origami turns an ordinary piece of paper into a beautiful creation. Anyone can do origami with some paper and patience. Do valley folds, mountain folds, and squash folds sound strange to you? Keep reading. Soon, these folds will make perfect sense. Use them to make fun and easy models like paper cups and fortune-tellers. Even if you've never tried origami before, soon you'll be surprising family and friends with your new skills.

Where Did Origami Come From?

In AD 550, the Japanese were first introduced to papermaking. Before long, the Japanese began folding paper in familiar shapes to entertain young children. The word "origami" comes from the Japanese words *oru* meaning "to fold" and *kami* meaning "paper." Through traveling magic shows, origami was introduced to the world. The craft caught on, and people young and old alike have enjoyed making origami ever since.

MATERIALS

Before you begin, take some time to choose your paper. Traditional origami paper can be found at craft stores, on the Internet, and in some bookstores. It's usually colored on one side and white on the other. But you don't have to use special origami paper. Almost any kind of paper can be used for origami. Notebook paper, newspapers, dollar bills, and wrapping paper all can be folded into fun shapes.

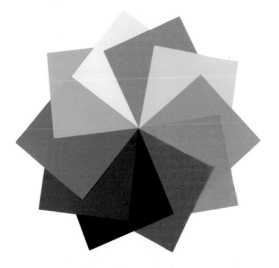

HOW TO USE THIS BOOK

Origami models are made with valley folds and mountain folds.
All other folds are just combinations of these two basic folds.

Valley folds are represented by a dashed line. The paper is creased along the line as the top surface of the paper is folded against itself like a book.

Mountain folds are represented by a pink dashed and dotted line. The paper is creased along the line and folded behind.

Reverse folds are made by opening a pocket slightly and folding the model inside itself along existing creases.

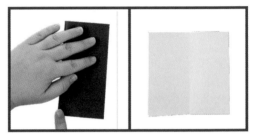

Mark folds are light folds used to make reference creases for a later step. Ideally, a mark fold will not be seen in the finished model.

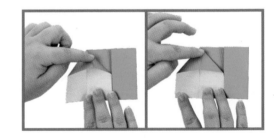

Squash folds are formed by lifting one edge of a pocket and reforming it so the spine gets flattened. The existing creases become new edges.

6

FOLDING SYMBOLS

A crease from a previous step.

Fold the paper in the direction of the arrow.

A fold or edge hidden under another layer of paper; also used as an imaginary extension of an existing line.

Fold the paper and then unfold it.

Turn the paper over or rotate it to a new position.

Fold the paper behind.

FOLDING 101: HOW TO MAKE A SQUARE

Most origami models are made from square sheets of paper. If you don't have square origami paper, don't worry. It's easy to make your own from any size paper. Here's how:

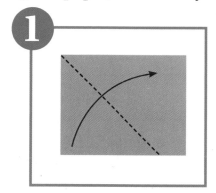

Fold the bottom left corner to the top edge.

Cut off the extra strip of paper.

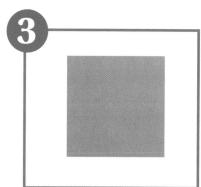

A finished square.

PAPER CUP

Traditional Model

The next time you head for the drinking fountain at school, bring a cup. All you need is a sheet of paper and a few simple folds. But drink fast. This paper cup won't last long!

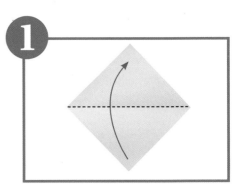

Start with the colored side down.
Valley fold in half.

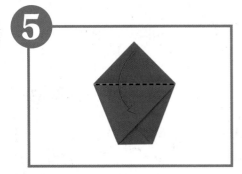

Mark fold the top right edge to the bottom edge and unfold.

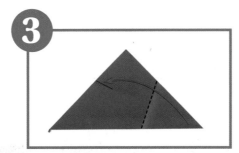

Valley fold the right corner to the mark made in step 2.

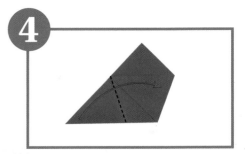

Valley fold the left corner to the right side.

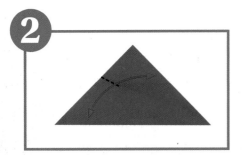

Valley fold the top layer.

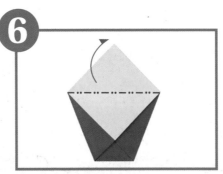

Mountain fold the remaining layer.

Finished paper cup.

Tea Time

These cups look like Asian teacups. Asian teacups come in different sizes. Small cups hold only one sip, while large bowl-sized cups are used in Japanese tea ceremonies. But unlike real teacups, paper cups should only be used for cold drinks.

SAMURAI HELMET

Traditional Model

Samurai warriors wore helmets called *kabuto* into battle. You could even make a *kabuto* that's large enough to wear. Just use a larger sheet of paper.

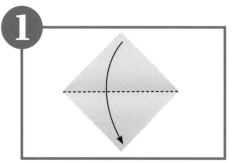

1

Start with the colored side down. Valley fold in half.

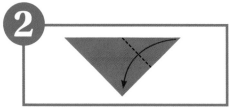

2

Valley fold the right corner to the bottom corner.

Children's Day

In Japan, young children make and wear samurai helmets on Children's Day. This day is celebrated on May 5. Families fly streamers and fish-shaped windsocks. The streamers represent whips samurai leaders carried into battle.

3

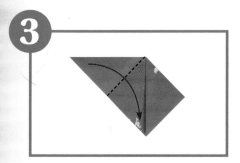

Repeat step 2 on the left side.

4

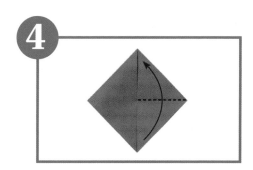

Valley fold the right flap to the top corner.

5

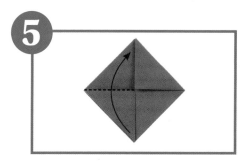

Repeat step 4 on the left side.

6

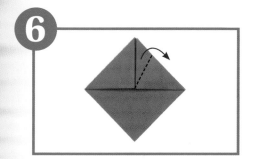

Valley fold the top tip to the right.

7

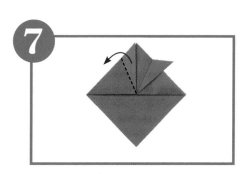

Repeat step 6 on the left side.

8

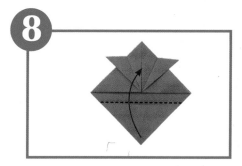

Valley fold the top layer.

9

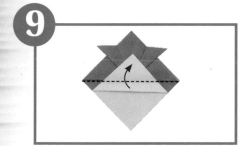

Valley fold along the bottom edge of the helmet to create the brim.

10

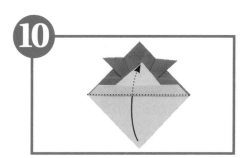

Valley fold the bottom corner into the helmet.

11

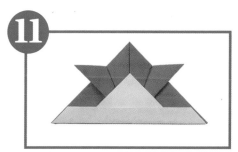

Finished samurai helmet.

HOUSE

Traditional Model

You can build your own mini home without bricks or nails. Use double-sided paper to create a colorful roof. The only thing left is to find a mini family to move in.

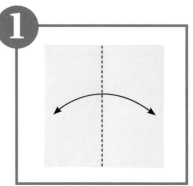

Start with the colored side down.
Valley fold in half and unfold.

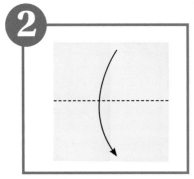

Valley fold in half.

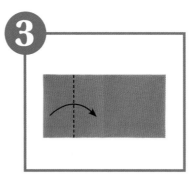

Valley fold the left side to the center crease.

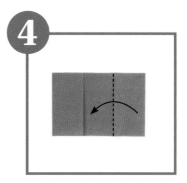

Repeat step 3 on the right side.

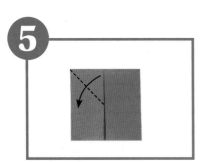

Valley fold the left side to the outside edge.

Repeat step 5 on the right side.

Squash fold the right side to create a roof.

8

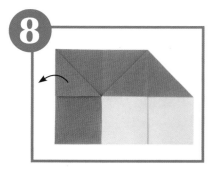

Repeat step 7 on the left side.

9

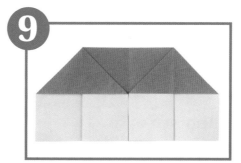

Finished house.

House Hints
Experiment in step 3 by changing the widths of the two roofs. Two narrow sides create barn silos or castle watch towers. Use smaller paper to make a mini doghouse or a birdhouse.

BANGER

Traditional Model

What's a party without a little noise? These bangers are a fun addition to any celebration. Make these noisemakers with ordinary notebook paper. Use a larger sheet of paper for a bigger bang.

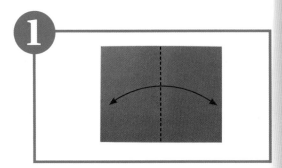

1 Start with a rectangular sheet of paper. Valley fold in half and unfold.

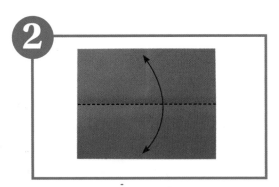

2 Valley fold in half and unfold.

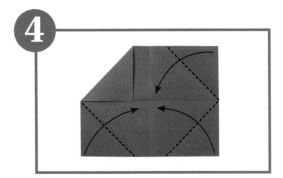

3 Valley fold to meet the crease made in step 2.

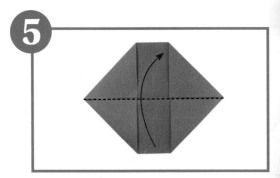

4 Repeat step 3 with the three remaining corners.

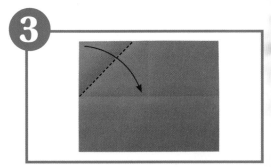

5 Valley fold in half.

14

How To Use

Hold the bottom two corners between your thumb and forefinger, with the single point facing your elbow. Quickly drop your arm down to create a "bang." Push the pocket back inside and repeat until your arm gets tired.

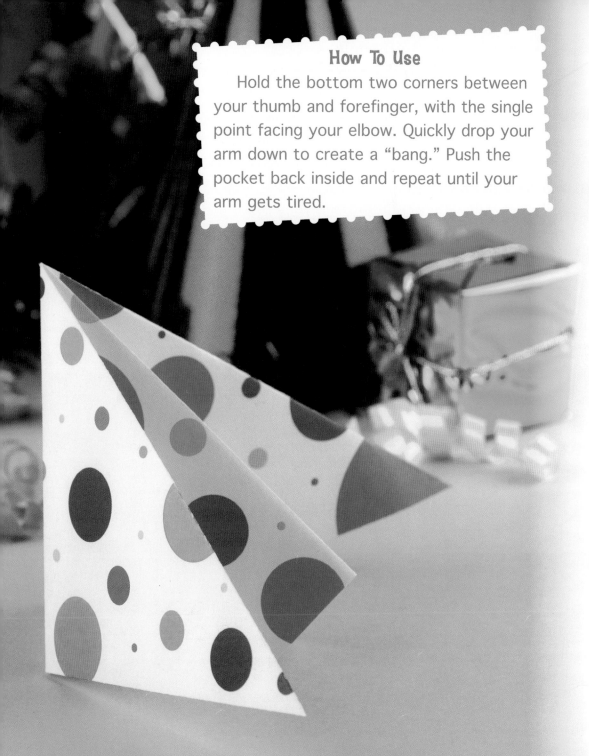

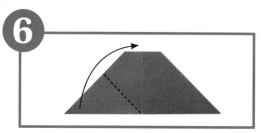

Valley fold the left side to the center crease.

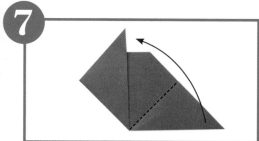

Repeat step 6 on the right side.

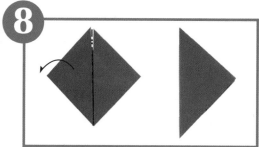

Mountain fold along the center crease.

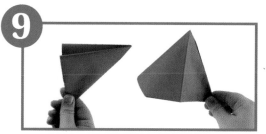

Finished banger.

SPACESHIP

Based on a model by Makoto Yamaguchi

Check out a model that's out of this world. This spaceship flies across tables when you blow into the back. Make two and challenge a friend to a space race.

1

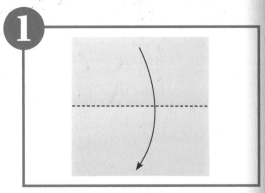

Start with the colored side down.
Valley fold in half.

2

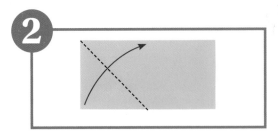

Valley fold the top layer to the top edge.

3

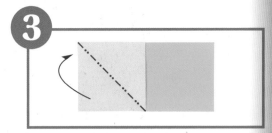

Mountain fold remaining layer.

4

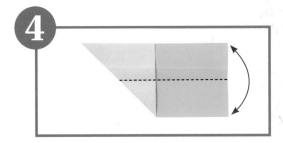

Mark fold in half and unfold.

5

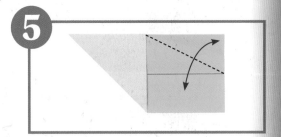

Valley fold from the triangle flap to the mark and unfold.

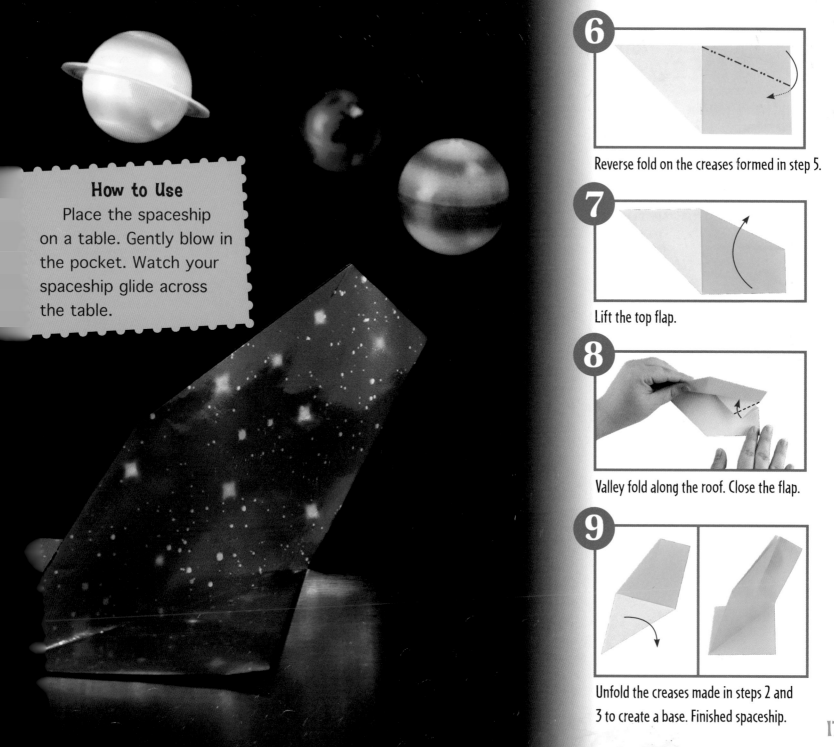

How to Use

Place the spaceship on a table. Gently blow in the pocket. Watch your spaceship glide across the table.

6

Reverse fold on the creases formed in step 5.

7

Lift the top flap.

8

Valley fold along the roof. Close the flap.

9

Unfold the creases made in steps 2 and 3 to create a base. Finished spaceship.

SPINNING TOP

Traditional Model

You'll need a big breath to make this top spin between your fingers. Use metallic paper for a shiny, strobe light effect.

1

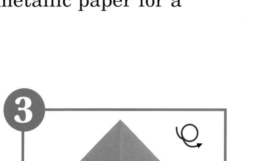

Start with the colored side up.
Valley fold in half and unfold.

2

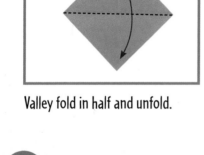

Valley fold in half and unfold.

3

Turn the paper over and rotate.

4

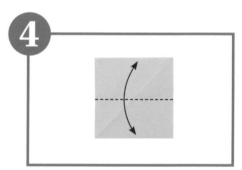

Valley fold in half and unfold.

5

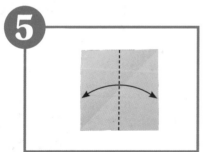

Valley fold in half and unfold.

6

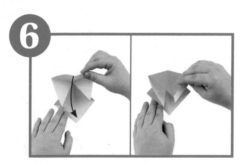

Squash fold.

7

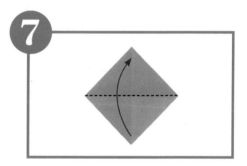

Valley fold the top layer.

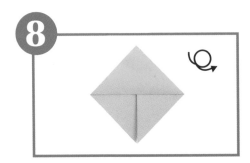

8

Turn the paper over and repeat step 7.

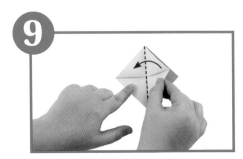

9

Valley fold the right side up.
Repeat behind.

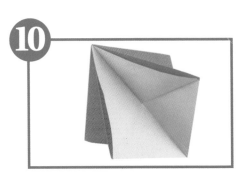

10

Finished spinning top.

How to Use
Loosely hold the tips between your fingers. Blow on the side and watch the top spin.

PYRAMID

Model designed by Mary Meinking

The Great Pyramid in Egypt was made using 2 million stone blocks. To make this miniature version, you only need a rectangular sheet of paper.

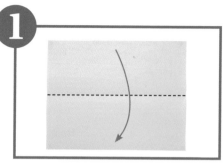

1

Start with a rectangular sheet of paper. Valley fold in half.

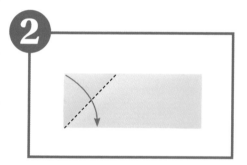

2

Mark fold the left side.

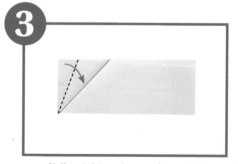

3

Valley fold to the mark made in step 2.

4

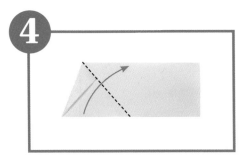

Valley fold to the top edge.

5

Valley fold to the bottom edge.

6

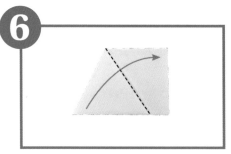

Valley fold to the top edge.

7

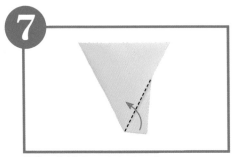

Valley fold the mini triangle.

8

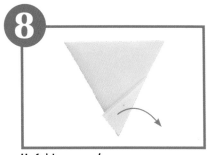

Unfold to step 4.

9

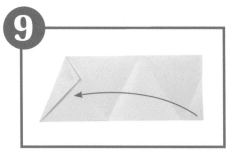

Tuck the corner into the pocket.

10

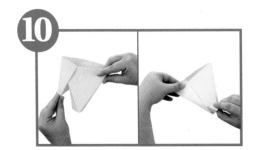

Push to form a snug edge on your pyramid.

11

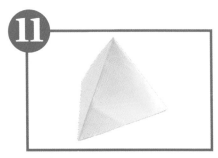

Finished pyramid.

Hidden Treasure

Your pyramid is fit for a pharaoh. Just like royalty, you can hide treasures inside your pyramid. Open the side flap to fill it with goodies. It's like being in Egypt without all the sand!

HEART

Traditional Model

This heart will make a great Valentine's Day card for someone special. Instead of buying boxed valentines, you could make these for all your friends and family.

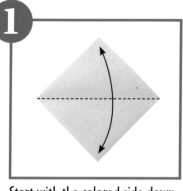

1 Start with the colored side down. Valley fold in half and unfold.

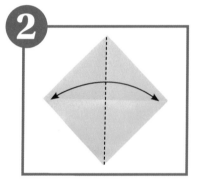

2 Valley fold in half and unfold.

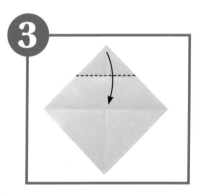

3 Valley fold to the center crease.

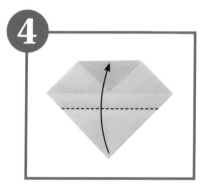

4 Valley fold to meet the top edge.

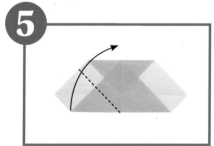

5 Valley fold the bottom edge to the center crease.

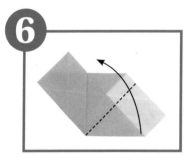

6 Repeat step 5 on the right side.

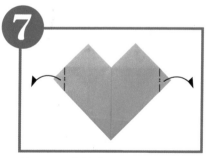

7 Mountain fold the corners.

Be My Valentine

Friends and loved ones have exchanged Valentine's Day cards since the 1400s. Except for Christmas cards, Americans exchange more Valentines than any other type of card.

Mountain fold the points.

Finished heart.

23

BUTTERFLY

Traditional Model

You can make a plain piece of paper come to life. This origami butterfly will flutter to the ground just like a real butterfly. The best part is you don't need a butterfly net to catch this one!

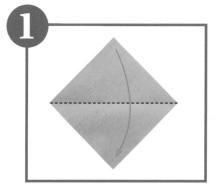

Start with the colored side down.
Valley fold the paper in half.

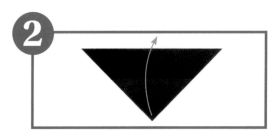

Valley fold past the top edge.

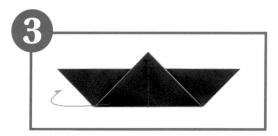

Mountain fold in half.

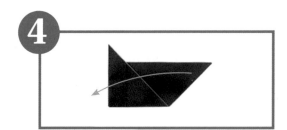

Valley fold the top layer to the left.

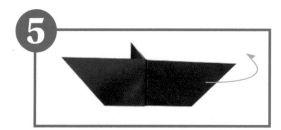

Mountain fold the right side.

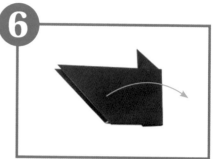

6

Lift up the two wings.

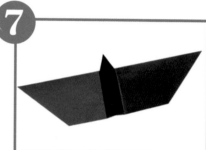

7

Finished butterfly.

How to Use

Point the triangle head of the butterfly forward and gently toss it in the air. Watch the butterfly flutter to the ground.

FORTUNE-TELLER

Traditional Origami

With this origami fortune-teller, your fortunes can be as serious or silly as you'd like. Gather a few friends and get ready to see what the future holds.

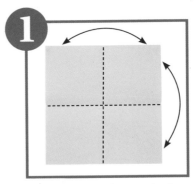

Start with the colored side down.
Valley fold in half both ways and unfold.

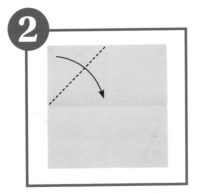

Valley fold the corner to the center.

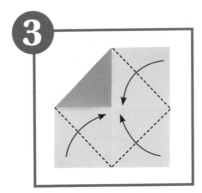

Repeat step 2 with remaining corners.

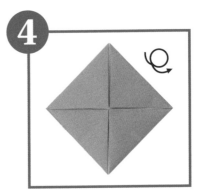

Turn the paper over and rotate.

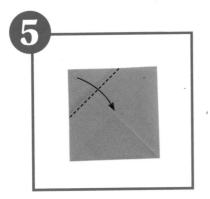

Valley fold the corner to the center.

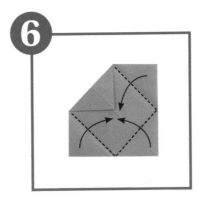

Repeat step 5 with the remaining corners.

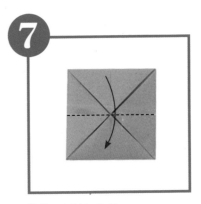

Valley fold in half.

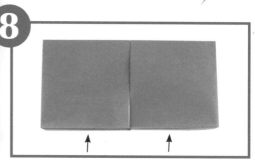

8

Push your thumbs and index fingers into each of the four bottom pockets.

9

Push up and to the center until the points meet and the pockets open.

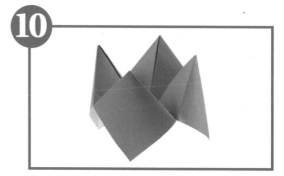

10

Finished fortune-teller.

How to Use

Flatten to step 7. Write different numbers or words on each of the eight small triangles. Lift the flaps to write fortunes on each of the eight triangles. Turn over. Write different colors on each of the four squares. Refold to step 9. Have a friend pick a color. With your fingers inside the pockets, open and close once for every letter. Then have your friend pick a number. Lift that flap to see your friend's fortune.

FUN FACTS

The artist/inventor Leonardo da Vinci was one of the first famous paper folders. He folded parchment into flying machines to understand the principles of flight. Many consider da Vinci the father of paper airplanes.

Akira Yoshizawa was a master origami folder. He created more than 50,000 origami models. He also created the international origami folding symbols of arrows and lines that folders still use today.

Origami is used for all types of advertising, including TV commercials. Origami has been found in commercials for cars, cat food, pizza, chocolate, and fast food restaurants.

The magician Harry Houdini amazed audiences when he folded paper into unusual shapes. In 1922, he wrote a book called *Houdini's Paper Magic*, which included four origami models. Turning ordinary paper into an extraordinary model is, after all, a magical process.

You don't need paper to fold origami. On cruise ships, towels are commonly used to fold lobsters, elephants, and other fun shapes. Room attendants leave these animals in passengers' rooms. When passengers return from dinner, they are often surprised to see these origami animals on their beds.

WHAT'S NEXT...

After completing the models in this book, you're ready to test your skills. The next book in this series is *Not-Quite-So-Easy Origami*.

In it, you'll learn how to make models like a trapdoor envelope, a hopping frog, and a flapping crane. These projects use the same folds you learned in this book. They have more steps, but with a little practice you'll master them in no time.

GLOSSARY

combination (KAHM-buh-nay-shun) — a mixture of two or more things together

crease (KREES) — to make lines or folds in something

flutter (FLUHT-ur) — to wave or flap rapidly

kabuto (kuh-BOO-toh) — a traditional helmet worn by samurai warriors

pharaoh (FAIR-oh) — a king of ancient Egypt

reverse (ri-VURSS) — opposite in position, order, or direction

samurai (SAM-oo-rye) — a Japanese warrior who lived long ago

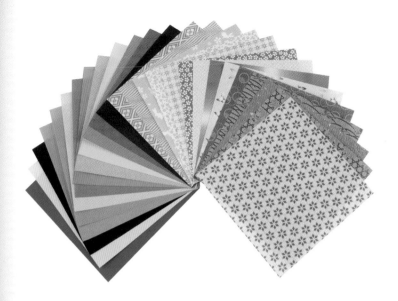

READ MORE

Boonyadhistarn, Thiranut. *Origami: The Fun and Funky Art of Paper Folding.* Crafts. Mankato, Minn.: Capstone Press, 2007.

Krier, Ann Kristen. *Totally Cool Origami Animals.* New York: Sterling, 2007.

Meinking, Mary. *Not-Quite-So-Easy Origami.* Origami. Mankato, Minn.: Capstone Press, 2009.

INTERNET SITES

FactHound offers a safe, fun way to find Internet sites related to this book. All of the sites on FactHound have been researched by our staff.

Here's how:
1. Visit *www.facthound.com*
2. Choose your grade level.
3. Type in this book ID **142962020X** for age-appropriate sites. You may also browse subjects by clicking on letters, or by clicking on pictures and words.
4. Click on the **Fetch It** button.

FactHound will fetch the best sites for you!

31

ABOUT THE AUTHOR

Mary Meinking grew up creating arts and crafts with her mother and two younger sisters. She took art classes where she drew and painted. Mary decided to turn her hobby into a profession. She studied art at the University of Kansas and has been a graphic artist ever since.

Mary shared her love for arts and crafts with her two children. Together they enjoy folding origami and paper airplanes. Mary has been published in 11 children's magazines and has written the book *Cash Crop to Cash Cow* (2009). She currently lives in Spirit Lake, Iowa.

INDEX